AMAZING ARCHITECTURE
AMAZING
ROLLER COASTERS

by Anita Nahta Amin

T0026243

Ideas for Parents and Teachers

Pogo Books let children practice reading informational text while introducing them to nonfiction features such as headings, labels, sidebars, maps, and diagrams, as well as a table of contents, glossary, and index.

Carefully leveled text with a strong photo match offers early fluent readers the support they need to succeed.

Before Reading

- "Walk" through the book and point out the various nonfiction features. Ask the student what purpose each feature serves.
- Look at the glossary together. Read and discuss the words.

Read the Book

- Have the child read the book independently.
- Invite him or her to list questions that arise from reading.

After Reading

- Discuss the child's questions. Talk about how he or she might find answers to those questions.
- Prompt the child to think more. Ask: Have you been on a roller coaster? What kind was it? What safety features did it have?

Pogo Books are published by Jump!
5357 Penn Avenue South
Minneapolis, MN 55419
www.jumplibrary.com

Copyright © 2023 Jump!
International copyright reserved in all countries.
No part of this book may be reproduced in any form without written permission from the publisher.

Library of Congress Cataloging-in-Publication Data

Names: Amin, Anita Nahta, author.
Title: Amazing roller coasters / by Anita Nahta Amin.
Description: Minneapolis: Jump!, Inc., [2023]
Series: Amazing architecture
Includes index. | Audience: Ages 7-10
Identifiers: LCCN 2022007792 (print)
LCCN 2022007793 (ebook)
ISBN 9781636907413 (hardcover)
ISBN 9781636907420 (paperback)
ISBN 9781636907437 (ebook)
Subjects: LCSH: Roller coasters—Juvenile literature.
Classification: LCC GV1860.R64 A45 2023 (print)
LCC GV1860.R64 (ebook) | DDC 791.06/8028—dc23
LC record available at https://lccn.loc.gov/2022007792
LC ebook record available at https://lccn.loc.gov/2022007793

Editor: Eliza Leahy
Designer: Molly Ballanger

Photo Credits: Doug Lemke/Shutterstock, cover; Cassiohabib/Shutterstock, 1; STUDIO MELANGE/Shutterstock, 3; photocritical/Shutterstock, 4; MasaPhoto/Shutterstock, 5; Future Publishing/Getty, 6-7; flyflyis/iStock, 8-9; zennie/iStock, 10; VIAVAL TOURS/Shutterstock, 11; aleksandr4300/Shutterstock, 12-13; umdash9/iStock, 14-15; Kritsana Laroque/Shutterstock, 16; Pit Stock/Shutterstock, 17; Various images/Shutterstock, 18-19; Tom Baracskai/Alamy, 20-21; ChameleonsEye/Shutterstock, 23.

Printed in the United States of America at Corporate Graphics in North Mankato, Minnesota.

TABLE OF CONTENTS

CHAPTER 1
A Safe Adventure 4

CHAPTER 2
Hold On Tight! 10

CHAPTER 3
Famous Roller Coasters 16

ACTIVITIES & TOOLS
Try This! 22
Glossary 23
Index 24
To Learn More 24

CHAPTER 1

A SAFE ADVENTURE

Have you ever been on a roller coaster? The Smiler in England seems to defy **gravity**! It has 14 loops.

loop

The Vanish coaster in Japan dives into an underwater tunnel. *Splash!*

Engineers design roller coasters. They follow strict rules. They make sure the rides are safe.

They make digital **models**. These show how the roller coasters will work. Then, construction workers build the coasters.

DID YOU KNOW?

After a coaster is built, sandbags or **dummies** ride it first. They ride in the cars just like people would. This tests if the ride is safe for people.

wheel

track

Each roller coaster car has wheels. Some wheels roll on top of the track. Some roll under it. This keeps the car from falling off. Wheels on the sides control turns.

How does the coaster stop? There are brakes on the track. **Sensors** control them. Brakes slow the cars down for certain parts, like when the ride is ending.

CHAPTER 2

HOLD ON TIGHT!

Roller coasters are fast! Hills help control their speed. Rolling down a hill makes a coaster go faster. Going up a hill slows it down. Many rides have a first big hill. A chain might pull the cars up. This is the cranking sound that some rides make.

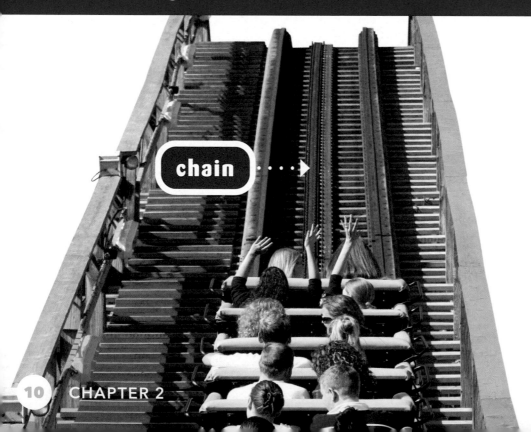

chain ····▶

Catapults push other rides up. At the top of the hill, gravity takes over. The cars roll down the hill. They get **energy** from this drop. It powers the rest of the ride. This is why the biggest hill is often at the start.

harness

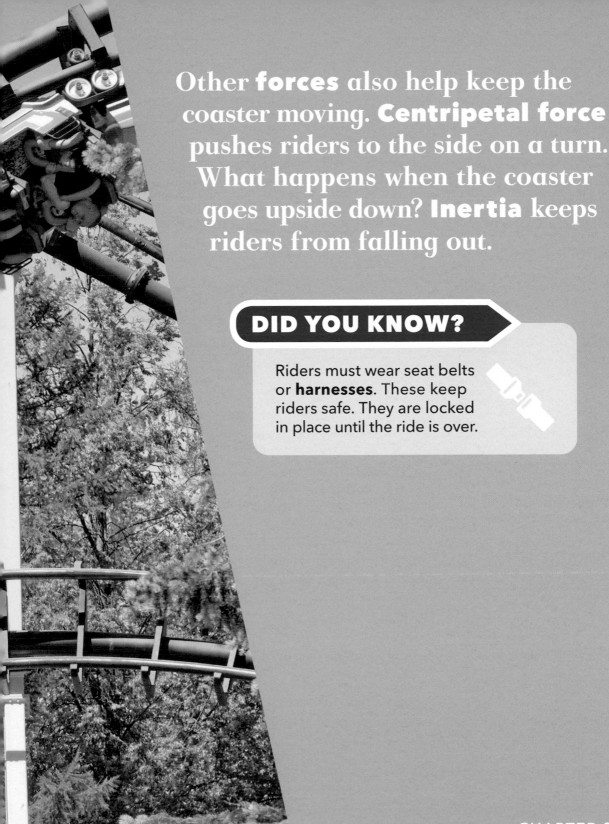

Other **forces** also help keep the coaster moving. **Centripetal force** pushes riders to the side on a turn. What happens when the coaster goes upside down? **Inertia** keeps riders from falling out.

DID YOU KNOW?

Riders must wear seat belts or **harnesses**. These keep riders safe. They are locked in place until the ride is over.

Gravity pushes the weight of the coaster and the people on it down on the track. **Supports** hold this weight. They are strong. There are many on each roller coaster. The weight pushes down to the **foundation**.

support ·····▶

TAKE A LOOK!

Centripetal force, inertia, and gravity are all at work on a roller coaster. Take a look!

= **CENTRIPETAL FORCE**   = **INERTIA**

= **GRAVITY**

CHAPTER 3

FAMOUS ROLLER COASTERS

Buckle up! The Formula Rossa in the United Arab Emirates has a catapult. This coaster goes 149 miles (240 kilometers) per hour. That is two times faster than a cheetah can run!

Kingda Ka is in New Jersey. A catapult sends it 456 feet (139 meters) in the air!

The Steel Dragon 2000 is in Japan. Its first hill is 318 feet (97 m) tall. It gets energy from this drop. This helps it finish the 1.5-mile (2.4-km) track.

DID YOU KNOW?

Roller coasters cost millions of dollars to build. The Steel Dragon 2000 cost $52 million!

$

The Gatekeeper in Ohio is a wing coaster. The seats stick out to the sides of the track. Riders' legs hang in the air. A steel **beam** holds each wing up. This ride has the highest upside-down point in the world. It is 170 feet (52 m) in the air!

Roller coasters are more than fun rides. Their designs are works of science!

ACTIVITIES & TOOLS

TRY THIS!

BUILD A ROLLER COASTER

Roller coasters get energy from going downhill. See how it works in this fun activity!

What You Need:
- ruler
- scissors
- cereal box
- tape
- marble

❶ Cut 1-inch-wide (2.5-centimeter-wide) strips of cardboard from the cereal box.

❷ Tape the ends together to make one long strip. Fold the strip lengthwise so there is an indent down the middle for the marble to roll in.

❸ Tape one end of the long strip to a flat surface.

❹ Bend the strip so it makes two hills, one big and one small.

❺ Tape the remaining end to the flat surface. You may also need to tape the strip between the two hills to keep it sturdy.

❻ Place the marble at the top of the first hill.

❼ Let go of the marble so it rolls down the hill. Does it have enough energy to make it up and over the second hill?

❽ Change the heights of the hills. What happens now? Experiment with twists. What do you notice?

GLOSSARY

beam: A long, thick piece of wood, concrete, or metal used as a support.

catapults: Tools used to launch things at high speeds.

centripetal force: A force that acts on an object that is moving on a circular path.

dummies: Models of people or objects.

energy: The ability of something to do work.

engineers: People who are specially trained to design and build machines or large structures.

forces: Actions that produce, stop, or change the shape or movement of objects.

foundation: A solid base on which a structure is built.

gravity: The force that pulls things toward the center of Earth and keeps them from floating away.

harnesses: Sets of straps used to connect people to something and keep them safe.

inertia: A property of objects that means they stay at rest or keep moving in the same way unless an outside force acts on them.

models: Things architects or engineers build or design as examples of larger structures.

sensors: Tools that can detect and measure changes and send the information to a controlling device.

supports: Structures that hold other things up.

Superman Escape, Australia

INDEX

brakes 9

build 6, 18

cars 6, 9, 10, 11

catapults 11, 16, 17

centripetal force 13, 15

chain 10

construction workers 6

engineers 6

Formula Rossa 16

foundation 14

Gatekeeper 21

gravity 4, 11, 14, 15

harnesses 13

hills 10, 11, 18

inertia 13, 15

Kingda Ka 17

loops 4

models 6

seat belts 13

Smiler 4

Steel Dragon 2000 18

supports 14

track 9, 14, 18, 21

Vanish 5

weight 14

wheels 9

TO LEARN MORE

Finding more information is as easy as 1, 2, 3.

❶ Go to www.factsurfer.com

❷ Enter "amazingrollercoasters" into the search box.

❸ Choose your book to see a list of websites.

FACT SURFER